GRAPHIC BIOGRAPHIES

ROSA PARKS

THE LIFE OF A CIVIL RIGHTS HEROINE

by
ROB SHONE

illustrated by
NICK SPENDER

Rosen Classroom Books & Materials™
New York

Published in 2007 by The Rosen Publishing Group, Inc.
29 East 21st Street, New York, NY 10010

Copyright © 2007 David West Books

First edition, 2007

Designed and produced by
David West Books

Editor: Dominique Crowley
Photo Research: Victoria Cook

Photo credits:
Pages 4/5 Library of Congress; pages 6/7 Library of Congress; page 44 top Library of Congress; page 44 bottom Carol Muse Evans, publisher, Birmingham Parent Magazine; page 45 top Carol Muse Evans, publisher, Birmingham Parent Magazine; page 45 bottom SIPA/REX FEATURES

Library of Congress Cataloging-in-Publication Data

Shone, Rob.
Rosa Parks: the life of a civil rights heroine / Rob Shone; illustrated by Nick Spender.—
1st ed. p. cm.
Includes index.
ISBN 10: 1-4042-0864-X (library binding)
ISBN 13: 978-1-4042-0864-3 (library binding)
ISBN 10: 1-4042-0927-1 (pbk.)
ISBN 13: 978-1-4042-0927-5 (pbk.)
6-Pack ISBN 10: 1-4042-0926-3
6-Pack ISBN 13: 978-1-4042-0926-8

1. Parks, Rosa, 1913—Juvenile literature. 2. African American women—Alabama—Montgomery—Biography—Juvenile literature. 3. African Americans—Alabama—Montgomery—Biography—Juvenile literature. 4. Civil rights workers—Alabama—Montgomery—Biography—Juvenile literature. 5. African Americans—Civil rights—Alabama—Montgomery—History—20th century—Juvenile literature. 6. Segregation in transportation—Alabama—Montgomery—History—20th century—Juvenile literature. 7. Montgomery (Ala.)—Race relations—Juvenile literature. 8. Montgomery (Ala.)—Biography—Juvenile literature. I. Spender, Nik. II. Title.
F334.M753P3867 2007
323.092—dc22

2006002735

Manufactured in China

CONTENTS

WHO'S WHO

Rosa Parks
(1913–2005) Rosa Parks, who was born Rosa Louise McCauley, spent her life fighting for civil rights and was the inspiration for the Montgomery Bus Boycott.

Edgar Nixon
(1899–1987) An official of the National Association for the Advancement of Colored People, Nixon became president of its Alabama branch.

Raymond Parks
(1903–1987) Raymond Parks, Rosa Parks's husband, was a barber from Tuskegee, Alabama. He supported his wife throughout her long civil rights career.

Martin Luther King Jr.
(1929–1968) Martin Luther King Jr. was the pastor of Montgomery's Dexter Avenue Church. He led the Montgomery Bus Boycott and, later, became a leader of the civil rights movement in America.

Ralph Abernathy
(1926–1990) With Nixon and King, Ralph Abernathy helped to organize the Bus Boycott. He worked closely with King during the 1960s civil rights movement.

Virginia Durr
(1903–1999) A great friend and supporter of Rosa Parks, Virginia Durr campaigned for women's rights and against racial injustice.

THE PAST

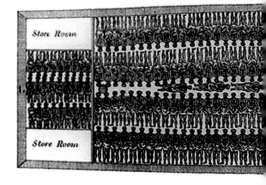

*O*n January 31, 1865, the U.S. Congress passed the Thirteenth Amendment. This amendment abolished slavery in the United States. Among the slaves freed in Alabama was a young boy named Sylvester Edwards, who would one day become the grandfather of civil rights pioneer Rosa Parks.

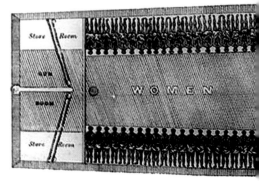

THE BEGINNING

In 1619, almost 250 years before Sylvester Edwards was given his freedom, a Dutch ship traded ten Africans for food at Jamestown, Virginia. Nineteen years later, Jamestown held the colony's first slave auction. The slave trade had officially begun on American soil.

TRADE

A triangular trade route was developed between America and the West Indies, Europe, and Africa. Raw goods, such as cotton from America, were traded for manufactured goods in Europe. The manufactured goods were sent to Africa and the West Indies and were exchanged for slaves, who farmed the cotton in America. The journey from Africa to America was called the Middle Passage. Captive Africans endured dire and often fatal conditions on the journey. In 1808, the Congress ended the trade in slaves.

LIFE AS A SLAVE

Life was hard for slaves. They were brutally beaten for any reason and sometimes legally killed, but this happened rarely as slaves were expensive. Conditions under slavery were shameful throughout America, with those on Southern plantations being the worst of all. Many slaves were injured, some even died.

HEAVY HARVESTING
Before modern machinery was introduced, slaves spent all day in the fields picking cotton by hand.

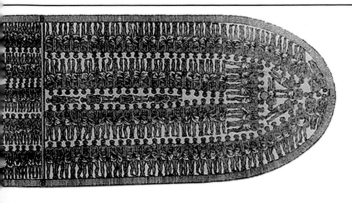

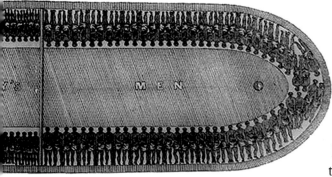

KING COTTON

In 1793, a man named Eli Whitney invented the cotton gin, a machine that picked out seeds from cotton. Only one slave was needed to operate the machine, which could do the work of dozens of people. America's cotton trade boomed. More and more cotton plantations sprang up, increasing the demand for slaves.

AN END TO SLAVERY

Early anti-slavery movements were formed in the North, where, little by little, slavery was banned. People in free states helped liberate Southern slaves via the Underground Railroad, a route by which slaves were smuggled to safety. Southern states saw the North as threatening their way of life. They felt the slave trade was vital, as slaves harvested cotton, which grew in the South and made the region prosperous. Fighting had already begun in Kansas, and the Southern states began to believe that withdrawal from the United States was the only way they could maintain their independence. Violence increased, and the Civil War had begun.

NIGHTMARE VOYAGES
At the height of the slave trade, a ship carried about 400 slaves. Sometimes, as many as 600 were crammed into the hold (the place where cargo is stored). Many slaves died during the journey.

THE DRED SCOTT CASE
In 1846, a slave named Dred Scott stood in a Missouri court and demanded his freedom. He had lived with his master in Illinois, where slavery had been abolished. Under Missouri law, he was entitled to be set free. The case lasted for over ten years. Eventually, Scott lost. The court said slaves were property, not citizens of the United States. As property, they had no legal rights. The case increased the tension between the North and the South.

LIVING WITH JIM CROW

A fter the North won the Civil War, Congress added new amendments to the Constitution. Southern states who had broken away from the union promised to follow this legislation in order to be readmitted.

RECONSTRUCTION OF THE SOUTH

The amendments gave new powers to African Americans. They stated that slavery must be abolished, gave civil rights to every person born in the United States, and made it illegal to deny anyone the right to vote based on race, color, or having been a former slave. Southern states promised to respect the changes, but they failed to do so. Before long, white supremacist groups such as the Ku Klux Klan began terrorizing blacks. The newly won rights of African Americans were quickly taken away.

REALITY
While new laws were supposed to give blacks freedom, blacks were kept powerless by white supremacists.

SEGREGATED SCHOOLS
Following the Plessy v. Ferguson *court ruling in 1896, segregated facilities were legal as long as they had the same resources. However, the "separate but equal" policy was rarely practiced. In 1954, the NAACP challenged this law in the* Brown v. Board of Education *case. The U.S. Supreme Court decided that a segregated school system was in itself unequal, and public schools were ordered to integrate. A cornerstone of segregation had been removed.*

African American schools often had fewer resources than all-white ones.

NOT TRULY FREE

Most freed slaves stayed with their former masters, doing the same work as they had done before, but for a tiny wage. Others became sharecroppers. They could grow their own crops but had to pay a proportion of their harvest to the landowner as rent. African Americans had won their rights, but remained in grinding poverty.

JIM CROW LAWS

Named after a nineteenth-century comedy character who mocked black people, Jim Crow was a system that separated whites from blacks. African Americans were forced to use different areas in all public places including restaurants, schools, cinemas, and even drinking fountains. One of the Jim Crow laws, in Montgomery, Alabama, required blacks to sit apart from whites on public buses. Facilities provided for African Americans were often grossly inferior to those provided for their white counterparts.

THE COLOR LINE
Even bus stations had separate waiting rooms for African Americans.

EARLY PIONEERS

Many people from different races challenged inequality. Booker T. Washington was a former slave who had become a college professor. He believed that education paved the way to wealth and equal opportunity.

W. E. B. Du Bois, an Atlanta University professor, thought that economic growth could only be achieved through political equality. He helped to found the National Association for the Advancement of Colored People (NAACP) in 1910. It was the first civil rights organization that tried to gain complete freedom for African Americans under the Constitution.

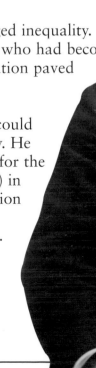

BOOKER T. WASHINGTON
Known as the "Great Accommodator," Washington believed that equality could only be gained gradually.

ROSA PARKS

THE LIFE OF A CIVIL RIGHTS HEROINE

1923, PINE LEVEL, ALABAMA. TEN-YEAR-OLD ROSA PARKS AND HER GRANDFATHER LISTENED TO THE SOUND OF KU KLUX KLAN HORSEMEN RIDING OUTSIDE.

DO YOU THINK THEY'LL GET IN HERE, GRANDPA?

IF THEY DO BREAK DOWN THAT DOOR, GRAB HOLD OF YOUR LITTLE BROTHER, AND RUN AWAY AS FAST YOU CAN.

MAYBE, MAYBE NOT, ROSA.

YES, GRANDPA.

THE RIDERS OF THE KLAN WERE A CONSTANT THREAT. NIGHT AFTER NIGHT, THEY TERRORIZED AFRICAN AMERICAN COMMUNITIES IN THE SOUTH.

THE KLAN SPREAD TERROR DURING THE NIGHT, BUT BY DAY THE YOUNG PARKS LOVED TO WANDER THROUGH THE PINE LEVEL WOODLANDS.

SHE HAD MOVED THERE WITH HER MOTHER, LEONA, AND YOUNGER BROTHER, SYLVESTER, FROM TUSKEGEE, ALABAMA WHEN SHE WAS FIVE YEARS OLD.

AS A CHILD, PARKS WAS OFTEN ILL. HER MOTHER TAUGHT HER AT HOME UNTIL SHE WAS WELL ENOUGH TO GO TO SCHOOL.

FOR AFRICAN AMERICAN CHILDREN, THE SCHOOL YEAR LASTED JUST FIVE MONTHS. DURING THE LONG SUMMER, THEY LEFT THEIR CLASSROOMS TO WORK IN THE COTTON FIELDS.

WHEN PARKS WAS ELEVEN, SHE WENT TO MISS WHITE'S INDUSTRIAL SCHOOL IN MONTGOMERY, ALABAMA. SHE LEARNED DISCIPLINE, SELF-IMPROVEMENT, AND A RANGE OF PRACTICAL SKILLS.

WHEN PARKS TURNED SIXTEEN, HOWEVER, SHE HAD TO LEAVE SCHOOL TO LOOK AFTER HER SICK MOTHER. BACK IN PINE LEVEL, A FRIEND INTRODUCED HER TO RAYMOND PARKS, A BARBER FROM TUSKEGEE.

WHAT DO YOU THINK OF RAYMOND, ROSA? DO YOU LIKE HIM?

WELL, I GUESS SO.

PARKS AND RAYMOND BEGAN SEEING EACH OTHER AS OFTEN AS THEY COULD. IN DECEMBER 1932, THEY WERE MARRIED AND MOVED TO MONTGOMERY, TAKING PARKS'S MOTHER WITH THEM.

SEGREGATION WAS STRICTLY OBSERVED IN MONTGOMERY.

RAYMOND WAS A MEMBER OF THE NAACP,* AND SOMETIMES MEETINGS WERE HELD AT PARKS'S HOME.

DID ANY KLAN MEMBERS SEE YOU COME IN?

I DON'T THINK SO.

*NATIONAL ASSOCIATION FOR THE ADVANCEMENT OF COLORED PEOPLE

PARKS KEPT WATCH OUTSIDE.

WHY SHOULD WE FEEL THREATENED? WE'RE NOT BREAKING THE LAW.

IN 1941, THE PARKSES MOVED TO CLEVELAND COURT IN MONTGOMERY. PARKS AND RAYMOND FOUND JOBS AT THE NEARBY MAXWELL AIR BASE. ALL U.S. MILITARY BASES WERE RACIALLY INTEGRATED.

OUTSIDE THE BASE, I'M TREATED LIKE A SECOND-CLASS CITIZEN, BUT HERE I'M AN EQUAL.

IN DECEMBER 1943, PARKS ATTENDED HER FIRST NAACP MEETING.

FIRST THINGS FIRST, WE NEED A NEW SECRETARY. ARE THERE ANY VOLUNTEERS? HOW ABOUT YOU, MRS. PARKS?

ME, MR. NIXON?

PARKS ACCEPTED THE POSITION. AS SECRETARY, SHE WORKED CLOSELY WITH EDGAR NIXON, PRESIDENT OF THE MONTGOMERY BRANCH OF THE NAACP. SHE HELPED TO FIGHT THE JIM CROW LAWS.

PARKS TRAVELED OFTEN THROUGHOUT ALABAMA TO INTERVIEW THE VICTIMS OF SEGREGATION.

OF ALL THE JIM CROW CUSTOMS, THE SEGREGATED BUSES WERE HATED THE MOST OF ALL. THE FRONT SEATS WERE FOR WHITE PASSENGERS ONLY. THE BACK SEATS WERE FOR AFRICAN AMERICANS.

AFRICAN AMERICANS HAD TO PAY AT THE FRONT, LEAVE THE BUS, AND THEN RE-ENTER USING THE DOOR AT THE REAR. WHEN A BUS BECAME FULL, THEY HAD TO GIVE UP THEIR SEATS TO WHITE PASSENGERS.

THE VOTING LAWS WERE ALSO DISLIKED. IN ALABAMA, WHITES MADE REGISTERING TO VOTE DIFFICULT FOR AFRICAN AMERICANS. IN 1943, PARKS TRIED TO REGISTER. AT THE CITY HALL...

BUT I HAVE A HIGH SCHOOL DIPLOMA!

YOU DIDN'T GET YOUR REGISTRATION CARD BECAUSE YOU FAILED THE LITERACY TEST.

FINALLY, IN 1944, PARKS BECAME A REGISTERED VOTER. FOUR YEARS LATER, SHE RESIGNED AS NAACP SECRETARY, BUT SHE STILL HELPED EDGAR NIXON RUN HIS OFFICE. ONE DAY, IN 1954...

ROSA, I'M GOING TO SEE CLIFFORD DURR. DO YOU WANT TO COME ALONG?

CLIFFORD DURR WAS AN ATTORNEY WHO WAS SYMPATHETIC TO THE NAACP'S CAUSE. IT WAS THROUGH NIXON THAT PARKS MET DURR'S WIFE, VIRGINIA.

MR. NIXON TELLS ME YOU'RE A GOOD SEAMSTRESS, MRS. PARKS. I HAVE A DRESS THAT NEEDS ALTERING.

PARKS DID THE WORK...

YOU'VE DONE A WONDERFUL JOB, AND, PLEASE, CALL ME VIRGINIA.

OH, I COULDN'T DO THAT, MRS. DURR.

THEN I SHALL JUST HAVE TO CALL YOU MRS. PARKS UNTIL YOU CHANGE YOUR MIND!

OVER THE YEARS, VIRGINIA DURR GAVE PARKS MUCH-NEEDED WORK, AND THE TWO WOMEN BECAME GOOD FRIENDS.

THE FOLLOWING SPRING, FIFTEEN-YEAR-OLD CLAUDETTE COLVIN WAS TOLD TO GIVE UP HER SEAT ON A BUS. SHE REFUSED...

...AND WAS ARRESTED.

PUT THE CUFFS ON HER!

NIXON SAW COLVIN'S CASE AS A CHANCE TO CHALLENGE THE JIM CROW BUS LAWS. HOWEVER...

THEY DROPPED THE SEGREGATION CHARGE AGAINST HER. WE CAN'T USE THE CASE.

ON DECEMBER 1, 1955, PARKS WENT TO THE MONTGOMERY FAIR DEPARTMENT STORE AS USUAL, WHERE SHE WORKED IN THE BASEMENT AS A TAILOR.

PARKS SPENT HER LUNCH BREAK WITH FRED GRAY, A YOUNG LAWYER AND ONE OF HER FRIENDS.

PARKS WORKED HARD ALL AFTERNOON.

AT 5:00 P.M., PARKS LEFT WORK. AFTER BUYING SOME CHRISTMAS GIFTS ON DEXTER AVENUE...

HO! HO! HO! MERRY CHRISTMAS!

...SHE CROSSED INTO COURT SQUARE TO WAIT FOR THE CLEVELAND AVENUE BUS.

CLEVELAN

2857

CLEVELA

PARKS SAT IN THE "COLORED" SECTION.

AT THE THIRD STOP...

DRIVER, YOU SEEM TO BE OUT OF SEATS BACK HERE.

DON'T WORRY. I'LL SOON FIX THAT.

YOU FOUR! I NEED THOSE SEATS, SO MOVE!

PARKS SAW THAT IT WAS JAMES BLAKE, THE SAME DRIVER WHO HAD THROWN HER OFF A BUS TWELVE YEARS EARLIER.

YOU HAD BETTER MAKE IT EASY ON YOURSELVES AND GIVE UP THOSE SEATS.

ARE YOU GOING TO STAND UP?

NO.

WELL, I'M GOING TO HAVE YOU ARRESTED.

YOU MAY DO THAT.

A FEW MINUTES LATER...

THERE SHE IS, OFFICER. ARREST HER!

I HEARD YOU WERE THIRSTY. HERE.

THANK YOU. THEY WOULDN'T LET ME HAVE A DRINK.

GET USED TO IT. THE GUARDS DON'T CARE ABOUT US. I SHOULD KNOW. I'VE BEEN IN HERE FOR NEARLY TWO MONTHS NOW.

THE POLICE WON'T LET ME PHONE ANYONE AND I DON'T HAVE THE MONEY FOR BAIL.

SOON AFTERWARD...

PARKS! YOU MAY MAKE THAT CALL NOW.

WHEN YOU'RE FREE, CALL THIS NUMBER AND TELL THEM WHERE I AM. PLEASE!

THAT NIGHT, NIXON CALLED FRED GRAY.

...SO THAT'S THE SITUATION, FRED. CAN YOU HELP?

FRED, I'VE BEEN WANTING TO TAKE ON THE BUS COMPANY FOR YEARS. LEAVE IT TO ME. I HAVE AN IDEA.

OF COURSE. I'D BE HAPPY TO TAKE ON ROSA'S CASE. LET ME CALL JO ANN ROBINSON. SHE'S A GOOD ORGANIZER.

JO ANN ROBINSON WAS A TEACHER AT ALABAMA UNIVERSITY AND A MEMBER OF THE WOMEN'S POLITICAL COUNCIL. AT MIDNIGHT, SHE WAS AT THE UNIVERSITY PRINTING HANDBILLS.

"ON FRIDAY, DECEMBER 2, 1955, THE WOMEN OF MONTGOMERY WILL CALL FOR A BOYCOTT OF THE CITY BUSES TO TAKE PLACE ON MONDAY, DECEMBER 5."

BY MORNING, 3,500 HANDBILLS HAD BEEN PRINTED. JO ANN ROBINSON CALLED EDGAR NIXON AND TOLD HIM OF HER PLAN.

THE BUS COMPANY MAKES MOST OF ITS MONEY FROM US, EDGAR. A ONE-DAY BOYCOTT WILL MAKE THEM SEE HOW IMPORTANT WE ARE. THEY'LL BE FORCED TO END SEGREGATION.

AFTER TALKING TO ROBINSON, NIXON CALLED HIS PASTOR, RALPH ABERNATHY.

IF THIS BOYCOTT IS GOING TO WORK, RALPH, WE NEED THE HELP OF THE LOCAL PASTORS. CAN YOU ARRANGE A MEETING?

FINALLY, NIXON CALLED JOE AZBELL, EDITOR OF THE "MONTGOMERY ADVERTISER." THEY MET AS NIXON WAS ON HIS WAY TO WORK.

THANK YOU FOR SEEING ME, MR. AZBELL. I'VE GOT A STORY I THINK YOU MIGHT LIKE TO PRINT.

MEANWHILE, PARKS ALSO HAD A CALL TO MAKE.

A FEW WEEKS LATER, SHE HEARD THAT HER CELLMATE OF THE PREVIOUS EVENING HAD BEEN FREED.

AT LUNCHTIME, PARKS WENT TO SEE FRED GRAY.

FRED! WHO ARE ALL THESE PEOPLE?

THEY'RE FROM "JET MAGAZINE," ROSA. THEY WANT TO TALK TO YOU.

THAT EVENING, AT THE CHURCH OF FUTURE CIVIL RIGHTS LEADER MARTIN LUTHER KING JR...

THANK YOU FOR ORGANIZING THIS MEETING, RALPH. WE'VE ADVERTISED THE BOYCOTT BUT WE STILL HAVE TO GET THE MESSAGE OUT TO PEOPLE IN THE CHURCHES THIS SUNDAY.

MANY OF THE PASTORS AREN'T SURE ABOUT THE BOYCOTT, EDGAR.

THE MEETING WAS NOT GOING WELL FOR THE BOYCOTT ORGANIZERS. THEN PARKS STOOD UP AND TOLD HER STORY.

...AND THAT'S WHAT HAPPENED.

EVERYONE AGREED TO SUPPORT PARKS AND THE BOYCOTT. ANOTHER MEETING WAS ARRANGED FOR MONDAY AT THE HOLT STREET CHURCH.

ON MONDAY MORNING, PARKS SET OFF FOR CITY HALL, WHERE HER TRIAL WAS TO BE HELD...

EMPTY!

ALL THE BUSES WERE EITHER EMPTY, OR NEARLY SO. THE BOYCOTT WAS A SUCCESS.

AT 9:30 A.M., PARKS ARRIVED AT CITY HALL.

THERE MUST BE A COUPLE OF HUNDRED PEOPLE, EDGAR. ARE THEY ALL HERE BECAUSE OF ME?

WHO ELSE?

THE TRIAL LASTED FIVE MINUTES. PARKS WAS FOUND GUILTY AND FINED $14.

THAT AFTERNOON, THE MONTGOMERY IMPROVEMENT ASSOCIATION (MIA) WAS FORMED TO ORGANIZE A LONGER BOYCOTT. MARTIN LUTHER KING WAS ELECTED AS ITS PRESIDENT.

WHY DID THEY PICK ME AS PRESIDENT, EDGAR? I'M NEW TO THE AREA.

IT'S **BECAUSE** YOU ARE NEW. YOU HAVE NO ENEMIES.

SEVEN THOUSAND PEOPLE TURNED UP FOR THE MEETING AT HOLT STREET CHURCH THAT NIGHT. THE NATIONAL PRESS WERE THERE, TOO.

THE MEETING STARTED AND MARTIN LUTHER KING STOOD UP TO SPEAK.

SINCE IT HAD TO HAPPEN, I'M HAPPY IT HAPPENED TO A PERSON LIKE ROSA PARKS, FOR NOBODY CAN DOUBT HER INTEGRITY OR HER CHARACTER.

BUT THERE COMES A TIME WHEN PEOPLE GET TIRED. TIRED OF BEING SEGREGATED AND HUMILIATED...

...TIRED OF BEING KICKED ABOUT BY THE BRUTAL FEET OF OPPRESSION. WE HAVE NO ALTERNATIVE BUT TO PROTEST.

FINALLY, RALPH ABERNATHY CALLED FOR A VOTE.

ALL THOSE IN FAVOR OF CONTINUING THE BOYCOTT, RAISE YOUR HAND.

THE WHOLE AUDIENCE VOTED FOR THE BOYCOTT TO CONTINUE.

31

TUESDAY, DECEMBER 7, 1955. SUPPORT FOR THE BOYCOTT WAS AS STRONG AS ON THE FIRST DAY.

TOGETHER THEY FORMED A CARPOOL. THE BOYCOTTERS WERE PICKED UP AND DRIVEN TO A PARKING LOT, WHERE THEY WAITED IN GROUPS.

MANY OF THE BOYCOTTERS OWNED CARS.

HOWE STREET? IT'S THE GROUP OVER THERE.

THEN, THEY WERE GIVEN A RIDE TO WHEREVER THEY NEEDED TO GO.

BACK AT CLEVELAND COURT...

YOU QUIT YOUR JOB?

I'M SORRY, ROSA. BUT HOW COULD I WORK IN A PLACE WHERE I COULDN'T EVEN SPEAK MY OWN WIFE'S NAME?

WHAT'S GOING TO HAPPEN NOW WITH BOTH OF YOU OUT OF WORK?

DON'T WORRY, MAMA. EVERYTHING WILL BE FINE.

RRRINNGGG!!
RRRINNGGG!!

I'LL GET THAT.

HELLO? WHO IS THIS? WHO IS...?

GASP!!

WHAT IS IT, ROSA? WHO WAS THAT? WHAT'S WRONG?

PARKS AND RAYMOND STARTED TO RECEIVE DEATH THREATS.

MEANWHILE, ALL ATTEMPTS TO BREAK THE BOYCOTT HAD FAILED. THE KU KLUX KLAN TURNED TO VANDALISM...

...AND VIOLENCE. ON JANUARY 30, 1956, AT MARTIN LUTHER KING'S DEXTER AVENUE HOME...

KAABOOOM!!!

NO ONE WAS HURT IN THE BLAST. IN THE COMING MONTHS, NIXON, ABERNATHY, AND OTHERS WOULD HAVE DYNAMITE THROWN AT THEIR HOMES, TOO.

DESPITE THE VIOLENCE, THE BOYCOTT CONTINUED. IN FEBRUARY, MIA FILED A LAWSUIT AGAINST THE MAYOR, CLAIMING THAT BUS SEGREGATION WAS UNCONSTITUTIONAL. THE BUS COMPANY OWNERS WERE WORRIED.

IF THIS BOYCOTT GOES ON MUCH LONGER IT COULD CLOSE US DOWN. WE'RE LOSING THOUSANDS OF DOLLARS A WEEK.

IT'S HURTING LOCAL BUSINESSES, TOO. PEOPLE AREN'T GOING TO THE DOWNTOWN STORES.

MONTGOMERY CITY LINES

THE CITY'S BUSINESSMEN JUST WANT THE BOYCOTT TO END. THEY DON'T CARE WHO WINS.

DON'T WORRY. THE MAYOR HAS SOMETHING PLANNED THAT WILL END THE BOYCOTT OVERNIGHT.

CITY OFFICIALS SOUGHT TO ARREST THE BOYCOTT'S ORGANIZERS. PARKS DID NOT WAIT TO BE ARRESTED, THOUGH.

I HEARD THAT YOU WERE LOOKING FOR ME.

SHE WAS FINGERPRINTED...

...AND PHOTOGRAPHED.

7053

THE WORLD PRESS HAD REPORTED PARKS'S ARREST. IN THE SPRING OF 1956, PARKS WENT ON A NATIONWIDE SPEAKING TOUR OF AMERICA TO RAISE FUNDS FOR THE BOYCOTT.

I'LL BE ABLE TO SEE SYLVESTER IN DETROIT. I DON'T KNOW HOW LONG I'LL BE GONE. LOOK AFTER MAMA FOR ME, RAYMOND.

PARKS SPENT A TIRING FOUR WEEKS SPEAKING AT NAACP MEETINGS...

...TALKING TO REPORTERS...

...AND APPEARING ON THE RADIO.

THEN, SHE FELL ILL.

YOU HAVE A STOMACH ULCER, MRS. PARKS. YOU NEED TO REST.

IN JUNE, PARKS CUT SHORT THE TOUR AND WENT BACK TO MONTGOMERY. THINGS WERE NOT HAPPY AT HOME.

I'VE BEEN GETTING THE CALLS EVERY DAY, ROSA. THE KLAN IS GOING TO KILL US BOTH!

MEANWHILE, CHARGES AGAINST ALL THE BOYCOTTERS, EXCEPT FOR THOSE AGAINST MARTIN LUTHER KING, HAD BEEN DROPPED. ON NOVEMBER 13, HE WAS BROUGHT TO TRIAL IN MONTGOMERY. AT THE SAME TIME MIA'S CASE AGAINST THE MAYOR WAS BEING HEARD IN THE SUPREME COURT. DURING A BREAK IN KING'S TRIAL...

IF WE LOSE THIS CASE, RALPH, IT COULD END THE BOYCOTT.

DR. KING, DR. KING! I THINK YOU SHOULD SEE THIS!

A REPORTER HANDED MARTIN LUTHER KING A NOTE. IT WAS THE SUPREME COURT DECISION.

IT'S OVER, RALPH.

WE WON.

THE SUPREME COURT HAD AGREED WITH THE MIA THAT BUS SEGREGATION WAS ILLEGAL. THE BOYCOTT CARRIED ON FOR ANOTHER MONTH UNTIL THE COURT ORDER WAS MADE OFFICIAL.

ON DECEMBER 21, 1956, 381 DAYS AFTER IT BEGAN, THE BOYCOTT ENDED. EARLY THAT MORNING, PARKS HAD VISITORS...

MRS. PARKS, I'M FROM "LOOK" MAGAZINE. I WAS WONDERING IF YOU COULD SPARE US A LITTLE OF YOUR TIME.

PARKS AND THE TWO JOURNALISTS WENT TO CLEVELAND AVENUE AND WAITED.

PARKS SPENT THE NEXT FEW HOURS RIDING THE CITY LINE BUSES AND HAVING HER PHOTOGRAPH TAKEN FOR THE MAGAZINE.

IT'S BLAKE! WELL, HE CAN'T HURT ME NOW.

IN AUGUST 1957, THE PARKSES LEFT MONTGOMERY FOR DETROIT. THE DEATH THREATS HAD BEEN INCREASING, AND RAYMOND'S HEALTH WAS SUFFERING. AT THE DETROIT RAILWAY STATION...

ROSA!

SYLVESTER!

IN DETROIT, LIFE WAS NOT EASY FOR THE PARKS FAMILY. RAYMOND FOUND IT HARD TO GET A JOB. HOWEVER, PARKS ENJOYED BABYSITTING HER NEPHEWS AND NIECES. SHE HAD NOT GIVEN UP HER LINKS WITH THE PROTEST MOVEMENT, THOUGH.

IN MARCH 1965, MARTIN LUTHER KING ORGANIZED A MARCH FROM SELMA, ALABAMA, TO MONTGOMERY TO PROTEST AGAINST THE VOTER REGISTRATION LAWS.

EVERYONE IS SO YOUNG. I DON'T SEE ANYONE I KNOW.

ROSA! OVER HERE!

BEFORE LONG, PARKS WAS AT THE HEAD OF THE MARCH WHERE SHE BELONGED, SIDE BY SIDE WITH RALPH ABERNATHY AND MARTIN LUTHER KING JR.

AS SHE MARCHED, OTHERS BEGAN TO RECOGNIZE HER, TOO.

ROSA! WALK WITH ME FOR A WHILE.

MRS. PARKS! IT'S GOOD TO SEE YOU AGAIN!

HELLO, ROSA!

ROSA!

MRS. PARKS!

THE END

THE STRUGGLE CONTINUES

Monday, December 1, 1975, was the twentieth anniversary of the Montgomery Bus Boycott. There was a huge celebration. When it was Rosa Parks's turn to address the crowd, she urged people to "keep on keeping on." The journey toward equal rights had begun, but equality for all had yet to be achieved.

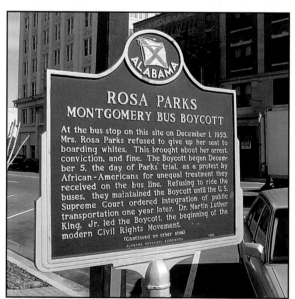

COURT SQUARE, MONTGOMERY
Parks's bravery has inspired many celebrities and public figures. Condoleezza Rice has said that she might not have become secretary of state without Rosa Parks's actions.

THE FRONT OF THE BUS
On December 21, 1956, Rosa Parks got on a Montgomery bus and sat at the front. Look *magazine recorded the event.*

EDUCATION
Parks said that education was one of the key tools in the struggle to end racism. She believed that by staying in school, young people have the chance to improve their own lives as well as those of others.

Education gives people an insight into the customs, lifestyles, and values of others, which leads to greater understanding. Learning about those whose race, religion, or nationality is different from yours is a way to end prejudice.

THE ROSA PARKS MUSEUM AND LIBRARY

This learning center at Montgomery University is built on the site where Parks boarded the bus, an action that changed history.

THE ROSA AND RAYMOND PARKS INSTITUTE

Founded in 1987 by Rosa Parks and close friend Elaine Steele, the Rosa and Raymond Parks Institute for Self-Development teaches about the civil rights movement.

It is famous for its "Pathways to Freedom" bus tours. These introduce people to important civil rights sites, including the Underground Railroad, through which slaves were smuggled to freedom. The center encourages those who take part in its programs to be respectful individuals, so that the world will be a better place for everyone.

A FINAL FAREWELL
Parks's body lay in state after she died on October 25, 2005. Usually, this treatment is only given to deceased politicians and military leaders.

GLOSSARY

abolish To put an end to.

amend Effect a change through an act of parliament or constitutional procedure.

auction A sale where the item being sold goes to the highest bidder.

boom A giant increase.

boycott A refusal to buy, use, or take part in something.

civil war A war where sides within a group fight each other. The American Civil War lasted from 1861 until 1865.

constitution The way in which a nation, state, or social group is governed, often recorded as a written document.

cornerstone A fundamental element.

discipline To punish.

entitle To deserve.

handbill A small, printed sheet of paper that is distributed by hand.

harass To annoy or worry a person repeatedly.

humiliate When a person is made to feel deeply embarrassed by another's unkind actions.

integrate To unite, instead of segregate.

integrity Sticking to a moral code of behavior.

Jim Crow A set of laws in the Southern U.S. that separated white and black people from each other.

legal Having to do with the law.

literacy Related to reading.

livestock Animals reared for food, profit, or pleasure.

loiter Hanging around without a useful purpose.

outriders Those who escort a large group of people, either on foot, on horseback, or in vehicles.

plantation An area designated for the growth of plants and trees.

political Related to politics and power.

protest To object strongly to something.

segregation The splitting off of a certain group from the rest of society.

sharecropper A farmer who works land owned by another person and receives tools and seeds on credit. The price of these is deducted from the sale of his crops when they are sold.

terrorize To instill fear and anxiety in another person.

thriving To be doing very well.

vandalism The destruction of property.

vital Absolutely necessary.

voyage A long journey with a specific purpose.